Burning the Bacon

To Mikey,
Make your mark on
the world. It's
waiting for you.
Cá, don't forget to
read a book or two)
Austen

l. austen johnson

Edited by: Aneesha Roy, Keertana Srinivasan
Consultant Editor: Morissa Schwartz

Illustrations: L. Austen Johnson, Ruxandra Șerbanoiu
Cover art by: Henry Baker
Cover and interior design by: L. Austen Johnson

GenZPublishing.org
Aberdeen, NJ

ISBN 13: 978-0692055496
ISBN 10: 0692055495

Contents

I. Gravity 5

II. In Memoriam 21

III. Entropy 37

IV. Parthenogenesis 54

1. Gravity

Gravity

Today I scribbled notes
On Einstein's general relativity.
The entire time,
I was just thinking
About you and me.
Stars and planets have gravity.
The greater the acceleration—
The larger the force—
The greater the gravity,
And therefore the slower time passes.
And to me it makes sense,
Because when I'm with you,
The gravity of our moments,
The weight of our smiles
Makes time nearly stop.

Anticipation

iktsuarpok (Inuit)
the feeling of anticipation
that leads you to keep
looking outside to see if anyone is coming

I got a letter in the mail,
the envelope as crisp as mid-winter air.
I opened it, and I swear,
I could smell your t-shirt, your blue-jeans,
your sheets—pine cones and fabric softener
and maybe, just maybe, a little bit of me.

I read your messy but deliberate
scrawl, random capitalization
and periods that were more
like crooked lines:
your words, saying you're finally,
finally, coming home.

After I put the folded sheet
back in its crisp capsule, every stroke
of the wind chime was really just you
whispering my name. The wind
made the cheap metal vibrate
after it had gone in fading waves.

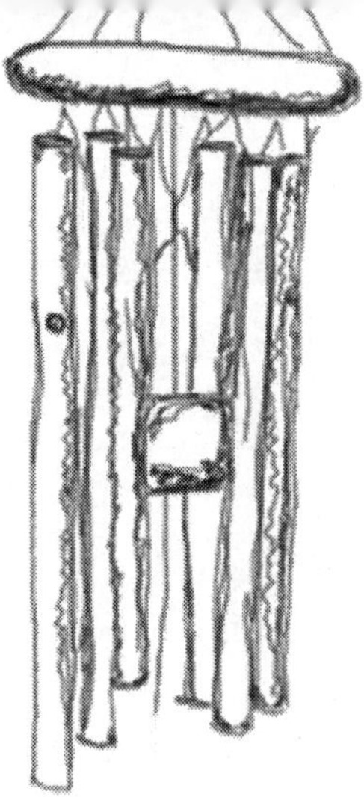

I turned the living room armchair around
to face the front walk. I couldn't focus
enough to sit, so my jitters drew up
alternative routes from laundry to kitchen,
pit-stops and divergences
to twist the once-short course into a quest
with the front-left window as a mid-way point
and my destination a moving target
somewhere outside its panes.

I may die from the waiting.

Burning the Bacon

I think I've inadvertently written an ode to you every
day since the one we met—you, self-assured and me,
suspicious. My dedication is the first breath
when I wake and the last before I close my eyes.
That's not to say I live for you. But in reading
the back of cereal boxes clearly designed for kids,
in running the tips of my fingers over the spine of
my favorite books (that whisper of kinetics),
in daydreaming and night jogging and burning the bacon
in that supposedly non-stick pan we bought at Costco,
of course I see at least a little bit of you.

When It Happens

You are not mine, exactly:
You are mine, inexactly.
There are five chambray shirts hanging in your closet,
and you gave me the smallest one to wear.
Can you imagine the feel of it?
Me, breathing in a bit of you,
and you, knowing it all was happening.

You once told me something I believed to be true:
"I'll know if you become my fire, my light, or my love."
But when it happens, you *won't* know.
I'll be in the kitchen browning the onions
and waiting for the chicken to bake.
You'll look over from your spot on the couch,
and smile at my cooking technique.

Perspective

"A woman waits
for me, she contains all, nothing is lacking,"
–Walt Whitman

I.
I wait for him,
Containing all,
for once
I am not lacking.

II.
I wait for her,
Containing all
(finally)
I am not lacking.

Habit

I double-check the dusty-gray gravel
   waiting outside my window,
   hoping that the gleam of light
   is really just snow
   that decided to grace us
   with its magic overnight.
It's a habit:
to look out the window
   in the middle of a wet winter
or to check the spot on the wall
   where a hook hangs from an old picture
   just to make sure it's not a bug
   (over and over again)
or to hold your hand
   when we walk
   from the blanketed park
   to our comfortered bed.
But soon it's a compulsion,
   something I can't escape.
You're a habit I keep repeating
   with no satisfaction.
You will be the last thing
   I see when I lay down to sleep.
You will be the first thing
   I glean in the morning.
You are my first and my last
   and sometimes too much in between,
and for that,
I hate you.
   (I hate me)
I think.

Dear John

When you ask me if you can kiss me,
and I say no, that's not
an invitation for you to keep trying.
I'm not a Magic 8 Ball
that you can just shake
until you get the answer you want.
I use you as an example
of a love horror-story.
I warn my friends about
any man that treats
them like you treated me.
To me you're
just another story to tell
in order to explain
why I'm so untrusting.
You're one of the people
my new dates say
they don't want to be.
They ask how you
could ever hurt someone else
like that, let alone me.
I tell them that I don't care,
I'm just not a fan
of history repeating.

Molded

I.
My body is changing shapes every day;
soon you will not recognize me.
Soon the part of me that bent to your shape
and sighed with your breath
will not exist,
and you will have to go on a hunt to find it.
You'll be disappointed,
but I'll be relieved.

II.
There is no place for naiveté in heartbreak,
but I forced it into every nook and cranny
that I could get my hands into.
It's there in the space between your ribs.
It's there in the creases of your eyes.
It's there in the spot you must have reserved
for me in the shadows of your mind.

III.
You will not recognize my body
after I have learned to love it.
You will search my personality
for the girl you once wasted some time with,
but she won't be there.

But you—you can never be metamorphosed out
of the hidey-holes of this thing I call my mind,
because like it or not,
the experience of us has shaped me.

And hate it or not,
this "new me" has been molded
with you in mind.

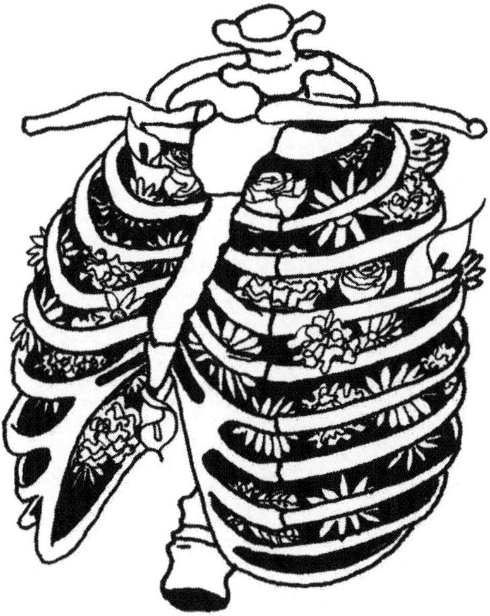

Optimism

Write a poem about escape.
About us:
My knobby knees curled up,
feet on the dash-
board, and you,
with your tanned hands
and perpetual smile
driving next to me,
too fast for my comfort,
but tame enough
that I can pretend
that I am safe.

Next time you hit your breaks,
I'll notice your glance,
lead-like eyes looking at me,
(maybe you just like looking;
maybe you're just worried:
This is what she's become?
Two love poems away
from a prison?
This is who she is now,
anxious and wavering.)

You told me everyone I meet
will fall in love with me.
I think of the great exception:
you.
I think of us driving,

and what I thought was a hopeful
prompt was really a catalyst
for the sharp pang
stab
pierce
of nostalgia.

With you, and your safe-heavy eyes,
and your sardonic sense of humor,
and, of course, your hands on the wheel.
And me with my bent knees
and my Catholic guilt,
and, of course, my optimism.
Who knew it wouldn't work out?

In the Room of First Heartbreak

After Ted Kooser

Here is a cookie-cutter house,
shaping us with drawn blinds
and closed quarters—laziness drapes over
our relationship like tennis shoes piled
string and rubber by string and rubber in the mud room.
There's no evidence of the dashing way
my heart should turn about when you're near
(metaphorical twist on metaphorical twist).
Over there sits the king-sized chair
with the burgundy suede that is really just one giant stain
and a drying rack, airing our
laundry, which is not quite dirty and
not yet considered fully clean. And here is
a surface easily scratched—like leather
and guitar backs and computer screens,
a little bit organic, a little bit manufactured—
that we called "us". But then there's the real
mess, all the stock-photo-filled picture frames,
unplanned "dinner and a movie"s on the kitchen calendar,
and indentations that your fingers might have left
(one after the other) on me. Of all the messy
things I have to clean, those I once anticipated
are the only ones that will make my heart throb
and my head sigh when I stop.

II. In Memoriam

Seriation

In Archaeology there's a way of dating
objects, trying to form relative
material order:
stratigraphic seriation.
The day I learned about categorizing ceramic
based on artistic style and chipped, ancient paint,
I went home and opened my bedroom door.

There it all was: our stratigraphy laid out.
There's a picture of us
on the dark-wooded desk hutch,
and a hole where another one used
to be pinned into the wall.
Your t-shirt is still mixed
in at the bottom of my laundry.
Your smile, still mixed
in with my memories.
There's a recent ticket stub buried
in the trash can next to my desk,
and one of your pencils is still submerged
in my art supplies.

Does this all make it easy to categorize
the reasons why you decided to leave
us in the past?
Here's the evidence overturned on the surface—
all my memories added up.

Nighttime Routine

I put oil in my hair, caress healing triptychs
of pump, lather, clean—such a comfort,
this falling asleep pretending to be a nymph.

I want to write that I haven't thought of you
recently, but I'm not in the habit
of lying to my pen. Listen,
I want to tell you that I think about you
every day, but I refuse to massage
false romanticism into my heart.

The rhythm comprising my hair routine
is not meant to be some great metaphor,
not a "I care for myself because you
certainly didn't care for me."
Maybe if I focus on healing the sun-damaged
strands (as if that's ever helped them in the past),
I won't focus on the list of films
that you collected, that we never
watched. I thought we would have time
to play the movies, resting on your tidy bed
and uncomfortable grey futon,

which is probably still sitting on the floor
in that same folded-up position, long after
I have stopped visiting.

Coming Back

Your house smells a little different
when you get back. Your cat meows
like she's offended you didn't call.
Something has surely broken. The upstairs
bathroom dwells in perpetual replacement.
The water is running. The TV is on.
Trying to count the number of times
the plants have been watered since you left
is easier than trying to count the blades
of grass in the yard where your favorite tree
has been cut down, but it's harder
than counting the number of tokens
still displayed on your cedar-coated shelf
from trips you didn't go on and places
you have never seen. This house is
a mausoleum of scratched-kneed and
rose-colored-lenses-wearing me.

Made in the Fields of Asphodel

My mother sits on the navy booth,
across from me.
My sister is squished on my right;
she chimes in,
"Pass the blue bread plate, please?"
as I'm tempted to take more than one—
Complimentary dinner rolls
are not to be trusted.
Buttery, fluffy, cheesy
or otherwise enticing,
they are a force to be reckoned with.
The sesame seeds on the top
of my dinner roll
call out like pomegranate seeds,
waiting to take me
into the realm of starchy Hell.
A vice turned my completely-non-guilty
pleasure. I figure,
We're all dying soon anyway,
so I say to my sister,
"Please pass the butter."

"Buttery Lobster Heaven at Luke's,"
reads the sign on the side of Route 29.
We've just passed a strip mall that I don't recognize
with stores whose names I do,

and two things run through my mind
upon reading the sign just outside of Luke's:
1) Gilmore Girls
2) If I could pick adjectives to describe my ideal heaven,
buttery and lobster-filled would both be
at the tippy-top of the list.

My mother passed her New England first loves
down, and while she's educated me
on lobster rolls, I've gotten her addicted
to sweet tea and the occasional biscuit.

It's a blistering ninety-three degrees,
and the leather of my car burns
worse on my thighs than if I had
let the sun walk me the whole way home.

My mother is not here, but I'd like her to be,
so we could pull over and park
and discuss our visions of heaven
and the maximum amount of lobster
we could comfortably eat
before we would need to sleep.

A Meal Abroad

We sit in what some would called a gastropub,
sharing a plate of baked camembert.
There's rosemary sprinkled on top of the cheese,
just like on our Christmas meat back home.
I drink a cup of English tea, while my dad
slices more pieces of bread.
Reaching for this shared plate,
I'm reminded of warmer winters.

Memory

When I was in 4th grade,
my homeroom class
was the special guest
of the Finnish embassy.
At that point, I barely
knew what an embassy
was, let alone that Finland
had one all to itself.

The embassy was
a Frank Lloyd Wright
type of masterpiece,
with clean lines that
did everything they could
to say, "This is
(not) a playground
for nine-year olds."

There we were:
fourteen little forms
walking in, adorned
in our best and finest,
shaking hands with
all the important people
that we passed
in bright, glassy halls.

Someone, maybe an intern,
ushered us into the basement,
and offered us candies
to eat that resembled
something like Skittles:
different flavors,
like the tropical sour packs,
and free of the 'S' branding.

We watched "Pelicanman"
without subtitles
but still managed to laugh
politely at all the important parts.
Of course, we didn't really
know what was happening–
I still don't really
understand it all today.

Bang, Click, Bang

Today I came home
for the first time in a long while.
The dryer now sounds like
machine gun fire,
and the stove smells far more like gas
than home cooking.
The drying machine door
keeps falling on the tiled
kitchen floor
(bang),
and I keep having
to put it back in place
(click).

So here I am in this big space
(bang)

all alone with a bang-click-bang
and a sharp echo.
It's so inconvenient
when the things you used to rely on,
like burners and dryers
and childhood houses
change or collapse.

Hair Dye

The last time I cried was over my hair.
It was over me not being able to communicate
and my body raging a war against my mind
that I thought could be fixed with hair dye.
Apparently, a chronic illness stays
even when my hair changes
from auburn to chocolate.
Pesky little things, those are,
hair colors and sickness.

Birthdays

My sister and I celebrate
our birthdays in tandem
every year in late October.
I remember my kindergarten year;
I had my party on her day.
She glared at me,
while I laughed with my friends
and petted the miniature-zoo
donkeys.

Now, she does not talk to me.
I sent her a gift in October,
and she sent back silence.
I should have known this would happen
when she told me all those years ago,
"You're the worst birthday present
I've ever gotten."

A house...

After Gregory Orr

A house just like her grandfather's
But made of words.
She doesn't remember everything,
But everything she remembers is inside it:
Red clogs and a loud typewriter,
And piles and piles of mail
For her mother.

Memories also—mysteries
And secrets.
A hallway that leads
To a floral couch for
The spirits,
An antennae'd
TV for the ghosts.
And, did I mention,
A hallway rotary phone?

Did I mention
That everyone she loves
But never knew
Lives there now,

In that poem,
In that ranch

Owned by someone new?

Time-capsule Shoebox.

"In past wars only homes burnt, but this time
Don't be surprised if even loneliness ignites.
In past wars only bodies burnt, but this time
Don't be surprised if even shadows ignite."
–Sahir Ludhianvi

I. There's a war going on everywhere
there's people. There's a war in your mind,
in your memories, in your front yard (split
on either side of the brick front-walk
like two armies in opposing trenches).
This front-door-slamming is really just a sign
that so-called political tactics
aren't welcome here.
Hint: You can lock the door. You can tear it down
hinge by creaky hinge.
Kick it down. Knock on the wood
until you get a splinter.
The siding is peeling, and it's really just a sign
that everything is breakable.

II. Quick! Pick one thing to take
as this house falls timber by timber.
Is it the trunk from elementary school
that sits at the end of your bed, unopened for years,
housing an archive of old Halloween costumes
and art projects? Or how about the first photograph
you took with the camera that your father gave you
when you told him it was time to try something new?

Hint: Either way some of your memories
will burn. Think of it in this way:
as a Viking funeral
or maybe the controlled burning
of a North American field in order to heal.
After your things turn to ashes, maize
will re-grow in a maze of lamppost-high stalks,
and your memories will walk in their shadows.

III. Will anything you try to save
actually be able to protect you
in this war that you're waging against yourself?
It's hard to hold the dogs at bay
when they know you.
It's harder to hold the enemy at bay
when it is you.
Do you hear Time's incessant knocking?
It's really just a figment of your imagination.
Hint: You know as well as I that Time
wouldn't let a door stop her.
As you choose your items
from this burning house of the past,
remember not to rush;
You will get out. Don't force it.

Resolution

I've pressed resolution
between our pages.
At one point, I thought
there was a story.
And yet, there wasn't enough
substance to preserve it.

III. Entropy

2nd Law

The second law of thermodynamics
says that entropy can only ever increase
in a closed system—
in other words,
physicists want us to believe
it's only ever going to get worse.

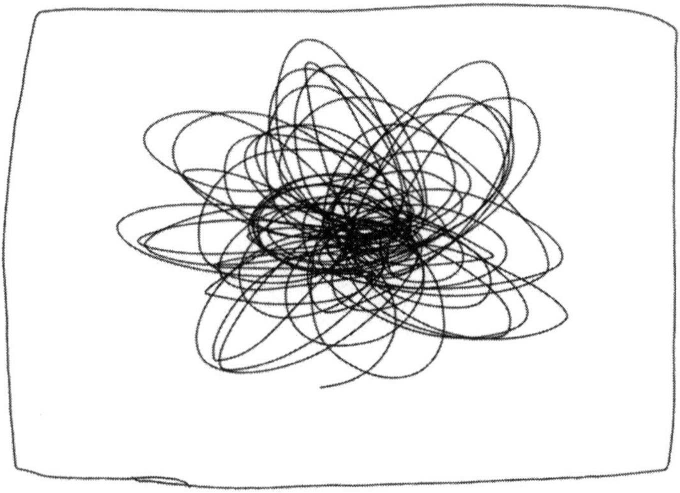

Known

There's a particular kind of embarrassment
that comes from being known by your pharmacist.
Steve The Pharmacist sees me
entirely through the lens of my antibiotics,
my pain reliever, and, most importantly,
my illness.
There's not enough interaction for me
to convince him that I exist as more
than a pill-popping robot, as more
than the lab results that "just got in," as more
than data and medical record numbers and
me always saying no to
"Do you have any questions for me today?"
Even though I do.
I want to ask if he knows what it's like
to be known like this—by what needs fixing.
To be known as broken, perpetually waiting
for that man-made thing that can actually repair me.
I can't survive without these pills, Steve,
so I guess that makes you my savior.

A Different Truth

Cf. "When Dreams Come True" by Leonid Afremov

The trees are rainbow, and the ground is slick
like most spring days have been so far this year.
We are hand-in-hand
passing empty, oversized benches and blooms
on this wide, cobblestone street.

Amidst the blue-purple and red-orange hues
of a violent, stormy spring,
marked by each passing, woven-metal street lamp,
and huddled in the part of the mind
that is reserved only for the memories
we want to tuck and fold and mold into art
like origami to hide their insides

is a moment we're turning our backs on.
Behind twisted cherry trunks
is two hours earlier, where,

in the spaces between silence,
lived crashing dishes
and midnight vacuuming,
which surely kept the neighbors up.
Let me tell you—
behind all this romanticism
is "Why don't I take the couch tonight?"
and then no reply. This is not
just an oil painting. We are not something complete
that you can mark with a little artist scrawl
that says the date
and the title.

Someone should have told you that already.

This is just a snapshot
of too many shades put together.
How jumbled it is, this cacophony
of our colors.

Lost

We're sitting at dinner;
you lean over
the already-cramped
table with your knife-
bright gleam of teeth
and shout, "You knew
this was going to happen!"
I try to make myself
smaller in my curved,
wooden chair.

"How could I
have known?"
I whisper,
hoping this
conversation
will end
soon.

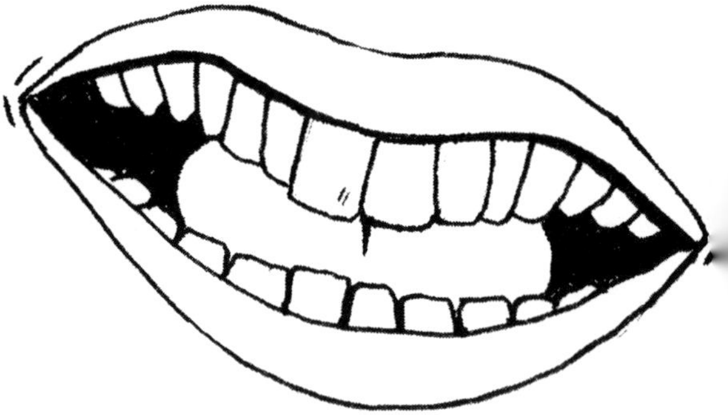

You lean back,
and the sky clears,
a black hue slicing through
the one round window
we have in our kitchen.
Then, your eyes soften.
Your hand retracts
from its spot by my cheek.
Your teeth tiptoe back
into their organized places.
You become human again.

Five years from now,
we'll be sitting at dinner,
you'll go on about how nice
it is that we don't have to feed
another mouth and besides,
"We're doing fine
on our own, aren't we, hon?"
I'll flash my knife-
sharp teeth, put
a little something
in my drink, and guzzle
down to the last drop.

Secrets, secrets are no fun
unless you share with everyone.

Light coasts along unfinished dry wall
and old boxes. A room so still
I could hear dust bunnies
strike at slices of shadow
that fall through the cracks
in the window shade.
The particles float in approximate corners
and fall from banisters
and tall, wooden shelving units,
which house neglected second editions.

Amidst the nearly-invisible spiders,
sailing under folded ladders,
and dodging packed-away
Christmas Tree decorations
is some painful bite of memory,
sticky with the inability to forget.

There is no photo album.
There is no newspaper clipping.
There are baby-sized gloves
and a broken-down crib,
with blue paint speckled on its otherwise
pristine exterior.

What my mother didn't tell me
is pressed between dainty
glass ornaments and pretty
repetition.

RLS

My body is revolting
against me, tossing limbs
and sharp, jointed corners
riled to frenzy,
roaring, "attend me
attend me."
I rise, at points,
with envy—what would
it feel like to sleep
through a night
with no turns, to
snuggle up with my bones,
to love my body
even when it's
revolting?

The Passion

Hallowed be Thy Name;
My name rages from your lips
tangible
molten in the space
between your silences
burning between breaths
Thy kingdom come,
I am afraid of night's
blistering stillness
and sweltering welts
Will the stars ignite me?
Ignite me
Thy will be done,
with a spark
Undo me
Do unto me
I am undone
I am undone
on earth as it is in heaven.
My heartbeat hollers,
Hallelujah
Hallelujah
You trade heaven
and earth for this?
Give us this day our daily bread,
Break your fast
with the curses
from my lips:
Devour me
Devour me

and forgive us our trespasses,
I'm sorry, I'm sorry, I'm sorry
I will break into pieces for you
I will shatter
if you ask
I have shattered before
but did you even blink
at my weeping?
as we forgive those who trespass against us;
Cauterize my edges
with the fire on your tongue
white-hot scars
on my heart
Speak only in tongues: Say,
Mend me
Burn me
and lead us not into temptation,
Consume me
Consume me
until there is nothing
but the bluest flame
that suffocates
but deliver us from evil.
until there is no air left
to scream
Amen.
your name

My Mouth

My mouth
My mouth
A monster in my mouth,
A spider has crawled
down my tongue
and is living in my throat,
and I cannot breathe

I want to tell someone
about the violence
living there,
lodged tight with
its many arms
and many legs,
but I cannot speak

I brush my teeth
far more often
than necessary,
hoping it will
make my mouth clean,
but the spider
does not crawl back out

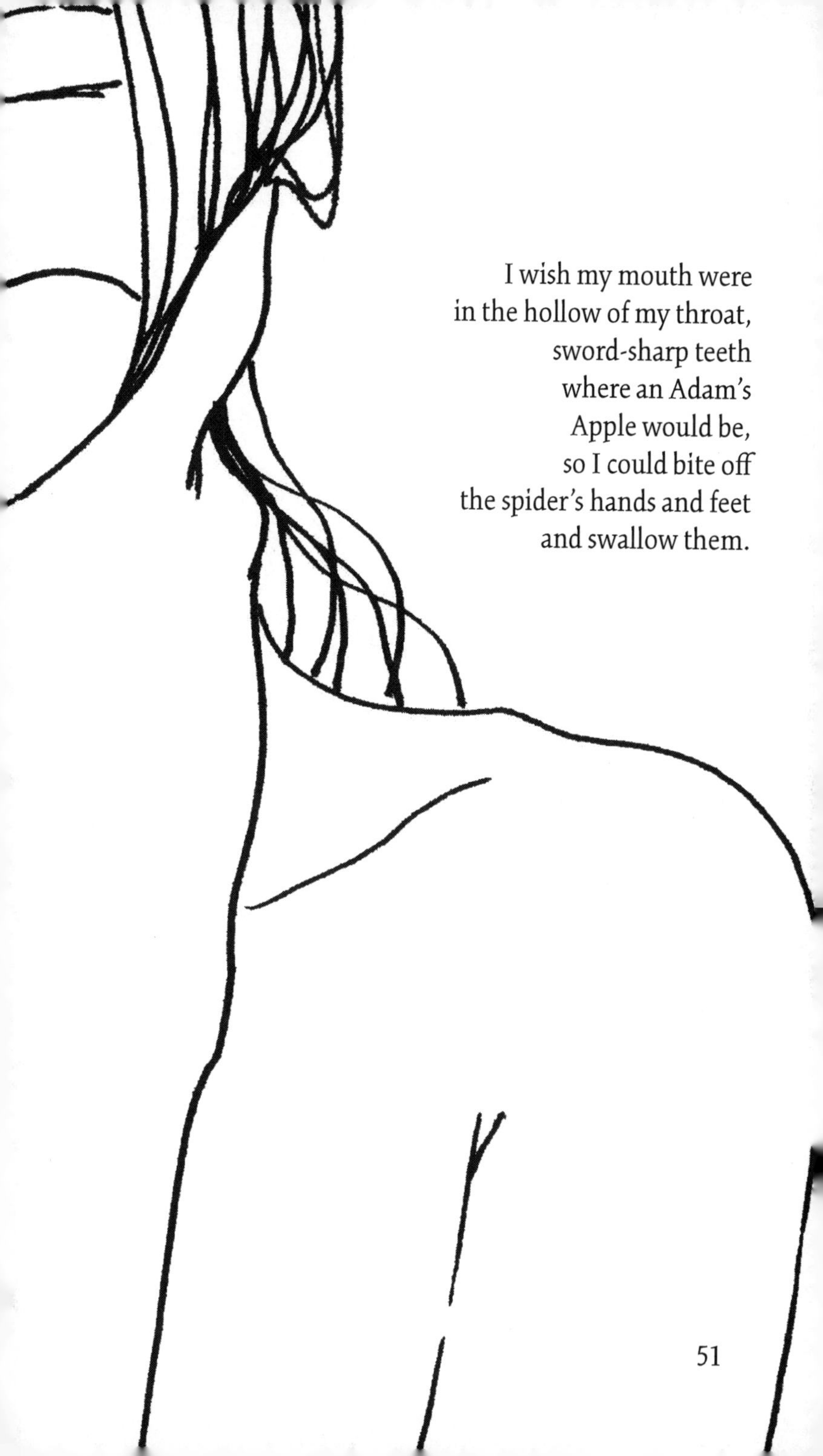

I wish my mouth were
in the hollow of my throat,
sword-sharp teeth
where an Adam's
Apple would be,
so I could bite off
the spider's hands and feet
and swallow them.

Being Alive

I.
Let me rip my sleeve and scratch my skin open
   to show you how my blood is organized.
It runs molten-hot over empty valleys
and coarse, calcium hills.
It flows through my sinew and does not burn it.
It peaks in my cheeks and flushes me pink.
You think me weak,
   because in my pale-grey wrists,
   my veins are a visible blue.
But do you see now, that I'm mortal lava?

II.
Prometheus breathed life into my body
   just after I was shaped,
   the great fire-tender and me
      (ember-lit clay and white ash).
For that, he was punished.
   Eagle by wretched eagle
   tore his insides out,
and Prometheus still did not repent.

Would you believe that he thought I was worth it?

III. Parthenogenesis

I will never hurt you

It is fall, and another year
appears in the yard.
The wonder of afternoon light
comes over us once again
as it creates a shadow play
through the holes in the leaves
that dance at our feet.

Here I am, I want to say:
Here I am,
my fingernails still soft,
my teeth still gentle.

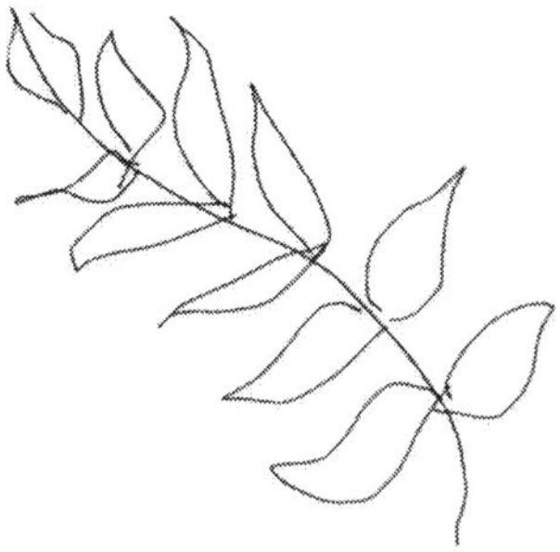

Thoughts at a Diner

I.
The closest I've ever come to therapy
is a 24-hour diner,
a salt shaker,
and this scrap of paper.

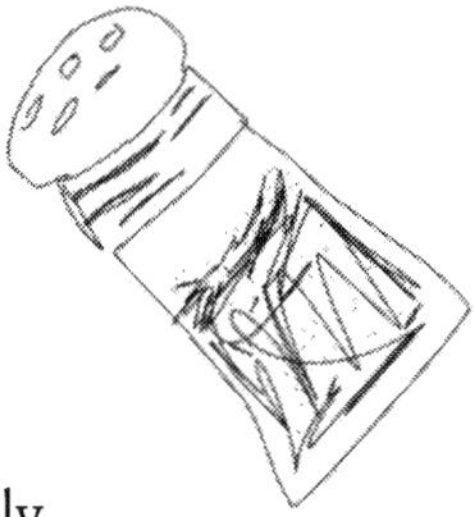

II.
Poetry to me is
my favorite pen
and whispered thoughts
that cower in the corner
until 2AM, when they suddenly
decide they love the spotlight.

III.
Restlessness is no longer a feeling;
it's a state of being,
my dogma, my will, my tonality.
I am nothing without fatigue.

IV.
This is the Obligatory War Story.
Except, I don't know war
other than my parents' arguments,
my own indecisive deliberations,
and what I choose to write.
But as I sit scribbling
on some crumpled
use-it-once-then-trash-it napkin
I think I deserve a penny
for my thoughts,

because, while I'm not killing
anyone to get them,
I've dug trenches in my mind
and put defensive mechanisms in my heart
that surely there's some medal for just living.

Blood is thicker than water
they say, and I guess
they're not wrong,
chemically speaking,
but water is more
transformative.
A baptism, a bath,
salt water on a wound,
or one hell of a
thunderstorm,
in which she
and I (of course)
came out the other side
brand new people.
I recall sitting
in an abandoned
treehouse for hours
waiting for that
boom, crackle, hiss
to pass over us,
and lo and behold,
we made it out
intact, and only a
little wet, saying,
look at our world,
cleansed, and
look at us anew too.

Sacrilegious Loving

I built an altar to myself
with bricks impressed
with *I am enough,*
with mortar of resilience.
This is sacrilege–
this power I have
to love myself,
this thing that dwells
deep in the reaches
of my twisted organs
and melodic veins.
That gift you gave;
those thoughts I stole.
Oh, sacrilegious loving.
Will I be enough?
There is blood on these stones
and scars on my soul
from cutting myself on the rock,
from working so hard to build–
sometimes carelessly,
sometimes in retrograde.
Don't you see its candles
in my liquid fire eyes?
Or the prayers
that whisper from my
sanguine lips, resounding?
Let me be enough.
Let me be enough today.

Cracks

Every morning
I break
my favorite mug,
coffee rushing
out from fissures
like the sea
around Moses
or the river
I almost drowned in
when I was young
and could not yet swim.

Every evening,
I glue the pieces
back together.
I tell myself,
if I didn't drown
then, why would
I break now?
Every day
I do not
crack open
my eggshell skin
or ceramic heart,
I mend.

On summer Sundays,
I eat peaches.
Or, I would if
I *could* eat peaches.
I listen to the sky
rain heaven down
on all our fields,
the Lord tangible
in the trees' lips
& the leaves' dewdrops.
I like to lie down
in the wet grass,
eyes closed,
water pounding,
& pretend
it's a baptism.

Holiday

Blackberry clouds
in a blue-blue sky,
we're sitting on one of those
red-white checkered
picnic blankets,
pretending we're on holiday.
Suddenly, the air
somersaults around us.
A gust of early autumn wind
slices between us.
My scarf runs away
with your hat.
You sit back
on your elbows,
and I cover my eyes
to protect from the
now-airborne dust.
I don't see the calm return.

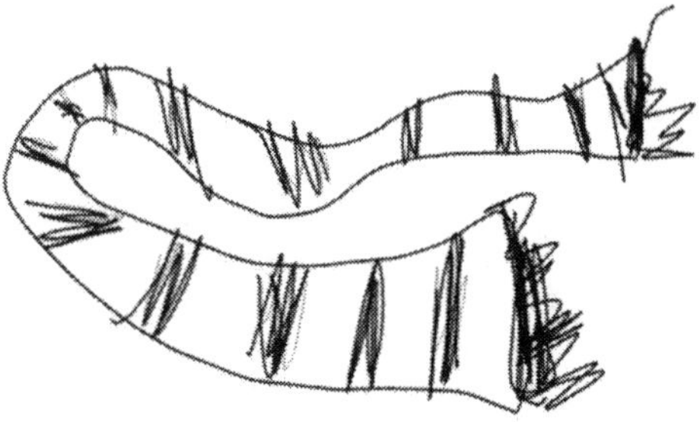

Thank you for taking the time to read my words. Your support means the world and more to me! I hope these words give you as much comfort to read as they gave me to write.

If you liked *Burning the Bacon*, please consider leaving a review. Scan the QR code below to find the book on Goodreads.

Acknowledgements

This collection would not be possible without my family, friends, and loved ones who were the first to read and support my work. Thank you for being my most sympathetic readers. Even if my pen runs dry, you'll be by my side. How lucky am I for that?

I am tremedously thankful for all the teachers and professors who have patiently helped me to wrangle my words, especially Gregory Orr, who showed me chaos and survival, and Herbert Tucker, who introduced me to the wordsmiths of the Victorian era and fueled my love for prosody.

Thank you also to *The Write Launch*, in which versions of "Anticipation" (as "Hope"), "Burning the Bacon," and "Lost" first appeared.

About the Author

L. Austen Johnson is a debut poet from Virginia and counts herself lucky to be from the lovers' state. She studied English, Archaeology, and Astronomy in university, which may explain her love for stargazing and time travelling.

She's an avid reader, a sometimes writer, and an attempter of various art projects. When she's not in class, you can find her searching for animals to pet, singing off-key in the shower, and learning the art of making the perfect cup of tea.

Connect with her on www.laustenjohnson.com, on Twitter @laustenjohnson, or on Goodreads, where she'd love to learn about her readers' favorite books.

THIS IS A GENZ PUBLISHING BOOK

GenZ™ is an innovative publisher for the new generation to have their work seen, recognized, published, and read by millions. We are on a mission to improve the world one word at a time. That is why we are the place for voices to be heard in a way not previously done in print or on digital media.

It can be nearly impossible for young writers with promising talent to produce standout work that will be recognized, because of the state of the publishing and digital media industries. Having work recognized in a sea of so many writers is even tougher. That is why there is an underrepresentation of young and innovative voices in the publishing and print world. There are many unheard voices. GenZ™ is on a mission to change that.

GenZ™ provides a medium where these people can be positively recognized for their work through a professional product and supportive company.

96371055R00041

Made in the USA
Columbia, SC
25 May 2018